Fatal Distractions: Conquering Destructive Temptations

Kay Arthur, David & BJ Lawson

PRECEPT MINISTRIES INTERNATIONAL

WATERBROOK
PRESS

FATAL DISTRACTIONS: CONQUERING DESTRUCTIVE TEMPTATIONS
PUBLISHED BY WATERBROOK PRESS
12265 Oracle Boulevard, Suite 200
Colorado Springs, Colorado 80921

All Scripture quotations are taken from the New American Standard Bible®. © Copyright
The Lockman Foundation 1960, 1962, 1963, 1968, 1971, 1972, 1973, 1975, 1977, 1995.
Used by permission. (www.Lockman.org).

ISBN 978-0-307-72981-1
ISBN 978-0-307-72982-8 (electronic)

Published in the United States by WaterBrook Multnomah, an imprint of the Crown Pub-
lishing Group, a division of Random House Inc., New York.

WATERBROOK and its deer colophon are registered trademarks of Random House Inc.

Printed in the United States of America
2012

10 9 8 7 6 5 4

SPECIAL SALES
Most WaterBrook Multnomah books are available at special quantity discounts when pur-
chased in bulk by corporations, organizations, and special-interest groups. Custom imprint-
ing or excerpting can also be done to fit special needs. For information, please e-mail
SpecialMarkets@WaterBrookMultnomah.com or call 1-800-603-7051.

CONTENTS

How to Use This Study v

Introduction: Fatal Distractions: Conquering Destructive
Temptations 1

Week One: Pride: Tripping Over Ourselves 5

Week Two: Anger: "I Do Not Have an Anger Issue!" 23

Week Three: Jealousy: "What's Yours Should Be Mine" 37

Week Four: Gluttony: "Let's Supersize That!" 51

Week Five: Slothfulness: "I'll Get to That Tomorrow" 69

Week Six: Greed: Chasing After More Than Enough 83

HOW TO USE THIS STUDY

This small-group study is for people who are interested in learning for themselves more about what the Bible says on various subjects, but who have only limited time to meet together. It's ideal, for example, for a lunch group at work, an early morning men's group, a young mothers' group meeting in a home, a Sunday-school class, or even family devotions. (It's also ideal for small groups that typically have longer meeting times—such as evening groups or Saturday morning groups—but want to devote only a portion of their time together to actual study, while reserving the rest for prayer, fellowship, or other activities.)

This book is designed so that all the group's participants will complete each lesson's study activities *at the same time*. Discussing your insights drawn from what God says about the subject reveals exciting, life-impacting truths.

Although it's a group study, you'll need a facilitator to lead the study and keep the discussion moving. (This person's function is *not* that of a lecturer or teacher. However, when this book is used in a Sunday-school class or similar setting, the teacher should feel free to lead more directly and to bring in other insights in addition to those provided in each week's lesson.)

If *you* are your group's facilitator, the leader, here are some helpful points for making your job easier:

- Go through the lesson and mark the text before you lead the group. This will give you increased familiarity with the material and will enable you to facilitate the group with greater ease. It may be easier for you to lead the group through the instructions for marking if you, as a leader, choose a specific color for each symbol you mark.

- As you lead the group, start at the beginning of the text and simply read it aloud in the order it appears in the lesson, including the "insight boxes," which appear throughout. Work through the lesson together, observing and discussing what you learn. As you read the Scripture verses, have the group say aloud the word they are marking in the text.

- The discussion questions are there simply to help you cover the material. As the class moves into the discussion, many times you will find that they will cover the questions on their own. Remember, the discussion questions are there to guide the group through the topic, not to squelch discussion.

- Remember how important it is for people to verbalize their answers and discoveries. This greatly strengthens their personal understanding of each week's lesson. Try to ensure that everyone has plenty of opportunity to contribute to each week's discussions.

- Keep the discussion moving. This may mean spending more time on some parts of the study than on others. If necessary, you should feel free to spread out a lesson over more than one session. However, remember that you don't want to slow the pace too much. It's much better to leave everyone "wanting more" than to have people dropping out because of declining interest.

- If the validity or accuracy of some of the answers seems questionable, you can gently and cheerfully remind the group to stay focused on the truth of the Scriptures. Your object is to learn what the Bible says, not to engage in human philosophy. Simply stick with the Scriptures and give God the opportunity to speak. His Word *is* truth (John 17:17)!

FATAL DISTRACTIONS: CONQUERING DESTRUCTIVE TEMPTATIONS

If you are a Christian, you have already made the most important decision of your life: you have surrendered your life to Christ! But you've probably discovered by now that the Christian life is not problem-free. Yes, you have the Holy Spirit living in you to provide guidance and strength, but you still struggle to live the way you know you should. This is because you are battling two enemies: Satan and yourself. Your nature was changed when you came to know Christ and He made His Spirit to dwell in you (1 John 4:13). But the Spirit dwells in a body of flesh, which is why you still find yourself struggling to do the right thing.

All of us commit individual acts of sin. But you may have noticed that certain sins seem to be more of a problem for you personally. Sometimes we wrestle with certain sin patterns or habitual sins—behaviors we fall into when we try to get our needs met apart from God. The source of that struggle is called *the flesh* or *the old man*. And if we live in the flesh rather than by the Spirit, these habitual sins will distract us from our pursuit of righteousness. They can literally kill our spiritual growth and keep us from maturing in our journey with Christ.

The early church identified a number of "capital sins"—the sins from which they believed most other sin originates. The church fathers named seven sins that are so corrupting, so evil and dangerous that for the last seventeen hundred years, they have been commonly called the seven deadly sins. And they are deadly—deadly to your spiritual growth. That is why we call them *Fatal Distractions*.

In this study we'll be identifying and discussing six of these seven deadly sins, sins that can distract you from nurturing your relationship with God and, left unchecked, can even be fatal to your spiritual journey: *pride, anger, jealousy, gluttony, slothfulness,* and *greed*. (We've decided to omit the seventh sin of *lust*, because we already have multiple Bible studies on the problem of sexual sin, including *The Truth About Sex* and the 40-Minute study *What Does the Bible Say About Sex?*)

As you learn more about these fatal distractions in the weeks ahead, we encourage you to ask God to help you identify, through His Holy Spirit, any subtle ways one or more of these sins has taken hold in your life and to help you conquer these destructive temptations, so that you can walk in victory with Him.

Of all the sins that can distract us from living effectively for Jesus, pride is one of the most insidious. It twists our perspective on the good gifts of God. We are tempted to believe that any successes or blessings come through our own efforts or depend on our own abilities. Pride takes our focus off God, and life becomes all about us, our accomplishments and goals.

This week as we consider what God says about pride, the first of our six fatal distractions, carefully examine your life for any evidence that this fatal distraction has taken root in your heart.

OBSERVE

Let's start by looking at Uzziah, a man whose life illustrates the way pride creeps into our thinking.

Leader: Read 2 Chronicles 26:3–5 aloud.

*• Have the group say aloud and draw a box around each reference to **Uzziah**, including pronouns:* ☐

As you read the text, it's helpful to have the group say the key words aloud as they mark them. This way everyone will be sure they are marking every occurrence of the word, including any synonymous words or phrases. Do this throughout the study.

2 CHRONICLES 26:3–5

3 Uzziah was sixteen years old when he became king, and he reigned fifty-two years in Jerusalem; and his mother's name was Jechiliah of Jerusalem.

4 He did right in the sight of the LORD according to all that his father Amaziah had done.

5 He continued to seek God in the days

of Zechariah, who had understanding through the vision of God; and as long as he sought the LORD, God prospered him.

2 CHRONICLES 26:16–21

16 But when he became strong, his heart was so proud that he acted corruptly, and he was unfaithful to the LORD his God, for he entered the temple of the LORD to burn incense on the altar of incense.

17 Then Azariah the priest entered after him and with him eighty priests of the LORD, valiant men.

18 They opposed Uzziah the king and said to him, "It is not for you, Uzziah, to burn

DISCUSS

• What did you learn about King Uzziah in this passage?

• What was his primary focus?

OBSERVE

After telling how God "marvelously helped" and strengthened Uzziah until "his fame spread afar" (26:15), the Bible describes a change in Uzziah's life.

Leader: Read 2 Chronicles 26:16–21 aloud. Have the group say and…
  • *draw a box around each reference to* **Uzziah,** *including pronouns.*
  • *mark the word* **proud** *with a* **P.**

DISCUSS

• What did you learn about Uzziah in this passage?

• Verse 16 starts with the word *but,* which shows that a contrast is about to take place. What contrast did you observe between these verses and the previous passage you read?

• When did Uzziah become proud? How did his pride affect his behavior?

• Discuss what he did wrong, according to verse 18, and how it was related to a pride issue.

• What does verse 19 suggest about the extent of King Uzziah's problem with pride?

incense to the LORD, but for the priests, the sons of Aaron who are consecrated to burn incense. Get out of the sanctuary, for you have been unfaithful and will have no honor from the LORD God."

19 But Uzziah, with a censer in his hand for burning incense, was enraged; and while he was enraged with the priests, the leprosy broke out on his forehead before the priests in the house of the LORD, beside the altar of incense.

20 Azariah the chief priest and all the priests looked at him, and behold, he was leprous on his forehead; and they hurried him out

of there, and he himself also hastened to get out because the LORD had smitten him.

21 King Uzziah was a leper to the day of his death; and he lived in a separate house, being a leper, for he was cut off from the house of the LORD. And Jotham his son was over the king's house judging the people of the land.

• Do these verses indicate that Uzziah repented? Explain your answer.

• Uzziah's distraction was subtle, almost undetectable. Pride took root in Uzziah's heart and eventually blossomed into out-and-out rebellion. If you ever were to find that same attitude in your own life, what would you do?

OBSERVE

Let's consider another Old Testament king who succumbed to the temptation of pride. God had saved King Hezekiah and Jerusalem from the Assyrian army. Many people brought gifts to the Lord and to Hezekiah—so many that other nations took notice of his exalted situation. Let's see what happened next.

Leader: Read 2 Chronicles 32:24–26 aloud.

Have the group say and...

- *draw a box around each reference to* **Hezekiah,** *including pronouns.*
- *mark each occurrence of the words* **proud** *and* **pride** *with a* **P.**

DISCUSS

- What did you learn about Hezekiah in verse 25?

- What consequences resulted from his attitude and actions?

- In what ways was his response to God's discipline different from King Uzziah's?

- What was the result of Hezekiah's response?

2 CHRONICLES 32:24–26

24 In those days Hezekiah became mortally ill; and he prayed to the LORD, and the LORD spoke to him and gave him a sign.

25 But Hezekiah gave no return for the benefit he received, because his heart was proud; therefore wrath came on him and on Judah and Jerusalem.

26 However, Hezekiah humbled the pride of his heart, both he and the inhabitants of Jerusalem, so that the wrath of the LORD did not come on them in the days of Hezekiah.

PROVERBS 8:13

The fear of the LORD is to hate evil; pride and arrogance and the evil way and the perverted mouth, I hate.

PROVERBS 6:16–19

16 There are six things which the LORD hates, yes, seven which are an abomination to Him:

17 Haughty eyes, a lying tongue, and hands that shed innocent blood,

18 a heart that devises wicked plans, feet that run rapidly to evil,

19 a false witness who utters lies, and one who spreads strife among brothers.

OBSERVE

We've already seen that God doesn't let pride go unnoticed. Let's see what more we can learn about His view of this sin.

Leader: Read aloud Proverbs 8:13; 6:16–19; and James 4:6.

> • *Have the group say and mark each reference to **pride**, including synonyms such as **haughty** and **arrogance**, with a **P.***

DISCUSS

• What does the Lord have to say about pride in these scriptures?

JAMES 4:6

But He gives a greater grace. Therefore it says, "God is opposed to the proud, but gives grace to the humble."

OBSERVE

The Bible is quite clear in its description of pride and warnings against its dangers. Let's look at a few more verses to see what we can learn about this fatal distraction.

PROVERBS 16:5

Everyone who is proud in heart is an abomination to the LORD; assuredly, he will not be unpunished.

Leader: Read aloud the following passages, from Proverbs 16:5 through 1 John 2:16.

- *Have the group say and mark every reference to* **pride,** *including synonyms such as* **haughty, arrogant,** *and* **boastful,** *with a* **P.**

PROVERBS 21:24

"Proud," "Haughty," "Scoffer," are his names, who acts with insolent pride.

ROMANS 12:16

DISCUSS

- What did you learn about the one who is proud from these verses?

Be of the same mind toward one another; do not be haughty in mind, but associate with the lowly. Do not be wise in your own estimation.

1 CORINTHIANS 13:4

Love is patient, love is kind and is not jealous; love does not brag and is not arrogant.

2 TIMOTHY 3:1–2, 5

1 But realize this, that in the last days difficult times will come.

2 For men will be lovers of self, lovers of money, boastful, arrogant, revilers, disobedient to parents, ungrateful, unholy…

5 holding to a form of godliness, although they have denied its power; avoid such men as these.

1 JOHN 2:16

For all that is in the world, the lust of the flesh and the lust of the eyes and the boastful pride of life, is not from the Father, but is from the world.

OBSERVE

What will happen to the one who is proud?

Leader: Read aloud Proverbs 15:25; 16:18; and Luke 1:51–52.

• *Have the group say and mark each occurrence of the words* **proud, pride,** *and* **haughty** *with a* **P.**

DISCUSS

• What will happen to the proud?

• Who will execute these things?

PROVERBS 15:25

The LORD will tear down the house of the proud, but He will establish the boundary of the widow.

PROVERBS 16:18

Pride goes before destruction, and a haughty spirit before stumbling.

LUKE 1:51–52

51 He [God] has done mighty deeds with His arm; He has scattered those who were proud in the thoughts of their heart.

52 He has brought down rulers from their thrones, and has exalted those who were humble.

OBSERVE

Self-righteousness goes hand in hand with pride. The Pharisees, for example, were proud of their detailed attention to keeping the law. They were extremely careful about such things as the foods they ate and ceremonial hand washing. However, Jesus taught His followers that external behaviors matter less than what's in our hearts.

MARK 7:20–23

20 And He [Jesus] was saying, "That which proceeds out of the man, that is what defiles the man.

21 "For from within, out of the heart of men, proceed the evil thoughts, fornications, thefts, murders, adulteries,

22 deeds of coveting and wickedness, as well as deceit, sensual-

Leader: Read Mark 7:20–23 aloud.

• *Have the group say aloud and mark the word* **pride** *with a* **P.**

DISCUSS

• What did you learn about pride from this passage?

• What types of behaviors did Jesus group together with pride, and what does this reveal about the seriousness of this sin?

OBSERVE

Throughout His ministry Jesus exposed the self-righteous attitudes of the Pharisees, who took such pride in believing themselves to be holier than others.

Leader: Read Luke 18:9–14 aloud. Have the group...

- *draw a box around each reference to the **Pharisee**, including pronouns.*
- *mark each reference to the **tax collector**, including pronouns and the phrase **this man**, with a dollar sign, like this: $*

DISCUSS

- What did you learn about the Pharisee?

- What did you learn about the tax collector?

ity, envy, slander, pride and foolishness.

23 "All these evil things proceed from within and defile the man."

LUKE 18:9–14

9 And He [Jesus] also told this parable to some people who trusted in themselves that they were righteous, and viewed others with contempt:

10 "Two men went up into the temple to pray, one a Pharisee and the other a tax collector.

11 "The Pharisee stood and was praying this to himself: 'God, I thank You that I am not like other people: swindlers, unjust,

adulterers, or even like this tax collector.

12 'I fast twice a week; I pay tithes of all that I get.'

13 "But the tax collector, standing some distance away, was even unwilling to lift up his eyes to heaven, but was beating his breast, saying, 'God, be merciful to me, the sinner!'

14 "I tell you, this man went to his house justified rather than the other; for everyone who exalts himself will be humbled, but he who humbles himself will be exalted."

• What difference(s) did you notice between the two?

• Discuss how pride can bring a halt to a person's spiritual growth.

• Pride causes us to emphasize self rather than God. Like the Pharisee, we begin to view ourselves as important. What is some evidence to watch for that may indicate pride has become an issue and needs to be dealt with?

• Examine yourself: who do you behave more like—the Pharisee or the tax collector?

OBSERVE

In light of God's view of pride, we need to know how to avoid it—and how to weed out any arrogance that has taken root in our lives.

Leader: Read aloud Proverbs 29:23; 1 Peter 5:5–6; Philippians 2:3–8; and Matthew 23:10–12. Have the group…

*• mark every reference to **pride**, including synonyms such as **empty conceit** and **exalts himself**, with a **P**.*

• draw a squiggly line like this ∿∿∿ *under each occurrence of the words **humble(d)** and **humility**.*

DISCUSS

• How is it possible to avoid or overcome pride?

• When it comes to overcoming pride, what one thing do all these scriptures have in common?

PROVERBS 29:23

A man's pride will bring him low, but a humble spirit will obtain honor.

1 PETER 5:5–6

5 You younger men, likewise, be subject to your elders; and all of you, clothe yourselves with humility toward one another, for God is opposed to the proud, but gives grace to the humble.

6 Therefore humble yourselves under the mighty hand of God, that He may exalt you at the proper time.

PHILIPPIANS 2:3–8

3 Do nothing from selfishness or empty conceit, but with humility of mind regard one another as more important than yourselves;

4 do not merely look out for your own personal interests, but also for the interests of others.

5 Have this attitude in yourselves which was also in Christ Jesus,

6 who, although He existed in the form of God, did not regard equality with God a thing to be grasped,

7 but emptied Himself, taking the form of

• Look for the word *but* in 1 Peter 5:5–6. What contrast is being made?

• What instructions did you find in these verses to guide us in dealing with pride?

• What will God do when we follow these instructions?

• From all you have seen in this week's lesson, have you identified areas in your own life where pride has crept in? In what ways, if any, has it become a distraction, keeping you from being as effective as you could be in your journey with Christ?

• Perhaps you realize that pride has invaded your life. What must you do to keep it from stunting or even killing your spiritual growth?

• By humbling yourself under God's hand, you are saying, "He is God and I am not." You acknowledge that everything good in your life—all you are and all you have and all you will accomplish—is a gift from Him. Are you ready in humility to trust Him with every area of your existence? Are you willing to submit yourself to Him?

a bond-servant, and being made in the likeness of men.

8 Being found in appearance as a man, He humbled Himself by becoming obedient to the point of death, even death on a cross.

MATTHEW 23:10–12

10 Do not be called leaders; for One is your Leader, that is, Christ.

11 But the greatest among you shall be your servant.

12 Whoever exalts himself shall be humbled; and whoever humbles himself shall be exalted.

WRAP IT UP

God has made it clear that He hates pride:

> The fear of the LORD is to hate evil;
>> Pride and arrogance and the evil way
>> And the perverted mouth, I hate. (Proverbs 8:13)

He knows the damage it can do to our lives and particularly to our relationship with Him.

Pride is one of Satan's favorite weapons of warfare because it causes us to take our eyes off God and place them on ourselves. This sin often creeps in unnoticed, in ways that seem benign, such as taking pride in the good things God has given us: family, jobs, influence, and success. If allowed to go unchecked, pride can change our attitude toward God and undermine our relationships with others.

Pride always overemphasizes self. It tempts us to believe we know better than God and that we can succeed apart from Him. Pride isolates us from God and keeps us from being totally devoted to Him. This fatal distraction kills our spiritual growth, preventing us from being fruitful in carrying out His plans and purposes for our lives.

By contrast, when we choose to clothe ourselves in humility, acknowledging God's authority and sovereignty in our lives, He will use us and exalt us in His own way and His own time.

This week:

- Ask God to examine your heart for any pride that might have crept in. If God shows you areas of pride, acknowledge it and

confess it. This may be difficult because often it has so cap-
tured your heart you may refuse to admit there is a problem.

- Ask God to forgive you for being prideful. (Make sure you say
  the word.)
- Pray that God would give you the ability and strength to turn
  away from pride. (Sometimes God does this through disap-
  pointment and brokenness. But remember He breaks us in
  order to bless us.)
- Ask God to give you the discernment to detect pride when it
  tries to creep into your life.
- Remember where you came from and how far God has brought
  you. Acknowledge your total dependence on Him, and thank
  Him for all that He has done in your life.

We live in the age of rage. Anger is on display everywhere: road rage, celebrity meltdowns, parents fighting at their children's athletic events, rampant lawsuits, and more. Our speech is filled with the language of anger: *That makes me so mad. I don't have to take this. Who do you think you are?*

This week let's consider how Christians should deal with anger in a culture that encourages us to demand justice when things don't go our way.

DISCUSS

Leader: Have the group briefly discuss their observations about today's epidemic of anger.

INSIGHT

Anger can be defined as "an internal, deep hostility aroused by something that displeases us."

OBSERVE

The "Wisdom" books of the Old Testament, particularly Proverbs and Ecclesiastes, draw some connections between wisdom and how we deal with anger.

PROVERBS 19:11

A man's discretion makes him slow to anger, and it is his glory to overlook a transgression.

PROVERBS 12:16

A fool's anger is known at once, but a prudent man conceals dishonor.

PROVERBS 14:29

He who is slow to anger has great understanding, but he who is quick-tempered exalts folly.

ECCLESIASTES 7:9

Do not be eager in your heart to be angry, for anger resides in the bosom of fools.

PROVERBS 29:8

Scorners set a city aflame, but wise men turn away anger.

Leader: *Read aloud the following passages, from Proverbs 19:11 through Proverbs 29:22.*

- *Have the group say aloud and mark each reference to* **anger**, *including synonyms such as* **quick-tempered** *and* **hot-tempered***, with an* **A.**

DISCUSS

- Discuss what you learned about anger in these verses.

- Several of these verses contrast two approaches to anger. Describe the different approaches and what each reveals about the people involved.

• How do you handle difficult situations?

PROVERBS 22:24–25

24 Do not associate with a man given to anger; or go with a hot-tempered man,

25 or you will learn his ways and find a snare for yourself.

• What about your friends? Are any of them hot tempered? If so, what is the danger for you in the relationship, according to Proverbs 22:24–25?

PROVERBS 29:22

An angry man stirs up strife, and a hot-tempered man abounds in transgression.

• Briefly describe a time when your anger led you to fight with someone, whether physically or verbally. What did it accomplish?

GALATIANS 5:16–17

16 But I say, walk by the Spirit, and you will not carry out the desire of the flesh.

17 For the flesh sets its desire against the Spirit, and the Spirit against the flesh; for these are in opposition to one another, so that you may not do the things that you please.

OBSERVE

We've seen that the wise person deals carefully with anger. But why is it often so difficult to control our tempers?

Leader: Read Galatians 5:16–17 aloud. Have the group...
- *draw a cloud shape like this* around each mention of **the Spirit.**
- *draw a box around each reference to* **the flesh:**

DISCUSS

- Discuss what you learned about the relationship between the Spirit and the flesh.

- How are believers to walk—to behave as a way of life?

- How does this relate to the topic of anger?

OBSERVE

The Spirit of God, who lives in every believer, and the flesh are at war with each other. They have different appetites—conflicting priorities—which leads to our internal struggle.

Leader: Read Galatians 5:19–21, 24–25 aloud. Have the group...
- *draw a cloud shape around each mention of **the Spirit**.*
- *draw a box around each reference to **the flesh:*** ▢
- *mark the word **anger** with an **A.***

DISCUSS

- What did you learn about outbursts of anger from this passage?

- What happens to those who practice anger as a way of life?

- If that is true, then what place does anger have in a believer's life?

GALATIANS 5:19–21, 24–25

19 Now the deeds of the flesh are evident, which are: immorality, impurity, sensuality,

20 idolatry, sorcery, enmities, strife, jealousy, outbursts of anger, disputes, dissensions, factions,

21 envying, drunkenness, carousing, and things like these, of which I forewarn you, just as I have forewarned you, that those who practice such things will not inherit the kingdom of God....

24 Now those who belong to Christ Jesus have crucified the flesh with its passions and desires.

25 If we live by the Spirit, let us also walk by the Spirit.

• How can we win the war against the flesh?

• What is to be the primary factor guiding the behavior of a believer?

COLOSSIANS 3:8–10

8 But now you also, put them all aside: anger, wrath, malice, slander, and abusive speech from your mouth.

9 Do not lie to one another, since you laid aside the old self with its evil practices,

10 and have put on the new self who is being renewed to a true knowledge according to the image of the One who created him.

OBSERVE

Leader: Read Colossians 3:8–10 aloud.

• *Have the group say and mark each reference to **anger,** including synonyms, with an **A.***

DISCUSS

• What do these verses instruct the believer to do in regard to anger?

• Why should we do this?

OBSERVE

"I do not have an anger issue!" Have you ever heard someone say that? Or perhaps you've said it yourself. How can you tell if you have a problem with anger, or if your response to a situation is normal and reasonable?

Leader: *Read aloud Psalm 55:3; Proverbs 29:22; and Hosea 7:6.*

• *Have the group say and mark each reference to **anger,** including synonyms, with an **A.***

DISCUSS

• From what you read, what does it look like when someone has an anger issue?

• Do you see any of these traits in your own life? If so, what do you need to do?

PSALM 55:3

Because of the voice of the enemy, because of the pressure of the wicked; for they bring down trouble upon me and in anger they bear a grudge against me.

PROVERBS 29:22

An angry man stirs up strife, and a hot-tempered man abounds in transgression.

HOSEA 7:6

For their hearts are like an oven as they approach their plotting; their anger smolders all night, in the morning it burns like a flaming fire.

GENESIS 4:3–8

³ So it came about in the course of time that Cain brought an offering to the LORD of the fruit of the ground.

⁴ Abel, on his part also brought of the firstlings of his flock and of their fat portions. And the LORD had regard for Abel and for his offering;

⁵ but for Cain and for his offering He [God] had no regard. So Cain became very angry and his countenance fell.

⁶ Then the LORD said to Cain, "Why are you angry? And why has your countenance fallen?

OBSERVE

Let's look at someone in the Bible who had an anger issue and see what effect it had.

Leader: Read Genesis 4:3–8 aloud. Have the group…
- *draw a box around each reference to Cain, including pronouns.*
- *mark the word angry with an A.*

DISCUSS

- What did you learn about Cain from this passage?

- Why was Cain angry, and what effect did his anger have on him?

• Was Cain the only one affected by his anger? Explain your answer.

7 "If you do well, will not your countenance be lifted up? And if you do not do well, sin is crouching at the door; and its desire is for you, but you must master it."

8 Cain told Abel his brother. And it came about when they were in the field, that Cain rose up against Abel his brother and killed him.

OBSERVE

Sometimes anger is a normal response to another person's sin. But how can we be sure we're handling our anger appropriately?

Leader: Read the following passages aloud.
  • *Have the group say and mark each reference to **anger**, including synonyms such as **wrath**, with an **A.***

JAMES 1:19–21

19 This you know, my beloved brethren. But everyone must be quick to hear, slow to speak and slow to anger;

20 for the anger of man does not achieve the righteousness of God.

21 Therefore, putting aside all filthiness and all that remains of wickedness, in humility receive the word implanted, which is able to save your souls.

PSALM 37:8

Cease from anger and forsake wrath; do not fret; it leads only to evildoing.

EPHESIANS 4:26, 31–32

26 Be angry, and yet do not sin; do not let the sun go down on your anger....

31 Let all bitterness and wrath and anger and clamor and slander be put away from you, along with all malice.

DISCUSS

• Discuss how anger is to be handled, according to what you've just read.

• According to James 1:19–21, what should be the characteristics of a believer? *quick to listen, slow to anger.*

• What warning about anger do you find in these verses? *it's not healthy & does not please God*

• What about you? Are you achieving the righteousness of God? *working on it*

• What did you learn about anger in Ephesians 4:26? *it's okay to be angry but do not sin*

• What are the implications of the instruction to "be angry, and yet do not sin"? *it's possible*

• Note the progression that starts with bitterness in Ephesians 4:31. Discuss the connection between each reaction and the next.

32 Be kind to one another, tenderhearted, forgiving each other, just as God in Christ also has forgiven you.

• Discuss the ways anger could become a fatal distraction in the life of a believer.

• In Ephesians 4:31–32 we aren't simply told to stop being angry; we're given a plan for overcoming our anger. What actions are we to take so that anger doesn't master us? *be kind, tender hearted forgiving each other*

• What truth in Ephesians 4:32 explains why anger should not be given full control in the life of a believer? *If God forgives us we should do the same to others*

• What is the connection between anger and unforgiveness? *when you are angry you cannot forgive others*

• Discuss some practical ways to get rid of anger and practice kindness and forgiveness.

remind myself the fruit of the spirit.

• How would handling your anger properly affect your relationships with both believers and unbelievers?

OBSERVE

In this next verse, the word translated as *wrath* is the same Greek word translated *anger* throughout our study.

ROMANS 12:19

Never take your own revenge, beloved, but leave room for the wrath of God, for it is written, "Vengeance is Mine, I will repay," says the Lord.

Leader: Read Romans 12:19 aloud.

   • *Have the group mark the words re-venge and wrath with an A.*

DISCUSS

• What truth did you learn about anger from this verse?

• How should this direct your response when others treat you unjustly?

WRAP IT UP

In and of itself, anger is not a sin. God gets angry at sin and injustice, and as His people, we should have the same reaction. Righteous anger can spark actions that bring about needed change and repentance. However, while God doesn't condemn anger, He does condemn the sins that result from misdirected or uncontrolled anger.

Anger is rarely the first emotion we feel in any given situation; instead, it arises out of other feelings prompted by some sort of conflict. For example, maybe you have been disappointed by shattered dreams or hurt by the unkindness of another person. When you embrace the emotions prompted by these situations, you may unknowingly open the door to anger. It is often easier to be angry rather than to deal with the initial emotions in a constructive way.

The problem is that uncontrolled anger damages us, and it damages those around us. The apostle Paul urged believers, "Be angry, and yet do not sin" (Ephesians 4:26). In other words, don't let anger control you. The longer you allow anger to continue, the greater the danger that you will sin and give Satan a foothold (Ephesians 4:27).

So what can you do when you feel anger taking control? Do you give in to it and spew it out on those around you, hoping to feel better once you have released it? Do you repeat, *I am not angry, I am not angry,* until the feeling goes away? Neither of these are the right solutions for the believer who wants to walk by the Spirit rather than be controlled by the flesh. Instead, here are some practical steps to take when you feel anger welling up inside:

1. Acknowledge your anger to yourself and to God.
2. Ask yourself why you are angry. Is this a righteous anger over sin, or are you just upset that things aren't going your way?
3. Step back from the situation and take a deep breath.
4. Ask the Spirit of God to take control and to help you keep calm and respond properly, leaving the revenge up to Him.
5. Ask God to help you show kindness, mercy, and forgiveness instead of reacting to what you feel.*

When you do this and leave the outcome in God's hands, you will be able to be angry and not sin. *Respond, don't react!*

Prayer Requests : Yvonne.

---

* For more on this subject, we recommend the 40-Minute Bible study *Forgiveness: Breaking the Power of the Past*. Anger can be both the result and the cause of bitterness. This study will teach you how to be set free from bitterness so that it will not control your life.

What takes place in your mind when you see someone with new clothes, a nice car, or an attractive spouse? What about when someone else gets the promotion or job you had hoped for? Choosing to be satisfied with what God gives us and where He's placed us isn't always as easy as it sounds. This week we'll take a look at jealousy, or envy, our third fatal distraction.

DISCUSS

Leader: *Open this week's lesson by asking the group to define jealousy.*

OBSERVE

Leader: *Read Proverbs 27:4 aloud.*
> • *Have the group say aloud and mark the word **jealousy** with a **J.***

DISCUSS

• What did you learn about jealousy and how it compares to wrath and anger?

PROVERBS 27:4

Wrath is fierce and anger is a flood, but who can stand before jealousy?

GALATIANS 5:19–21

19 Now the deeds of the flesh are evident, which are: immorality, impurity, sensuality,

20 idolatry, sorcery, enmities, strife, jealousy, outbursts of anger, disputes, dissensions, factions,

21 envying, drunkenness, carousing, and things like these, of which I forewarn you, just as I have forewarned you, that those who practice such things will not inherit the kingdom of God.

ROMANS 13:13–14

13 Let us behave properly as in the day, not in carousing and drunkenness, not in

OBSERVE

What is jealousy, or envy? What is its source?

when you want what others have

Leader: Read aloud Galatians 5:19–21; Romans 13:13–14; and Titus 3:3–5.

> • *Have the group say and mark each reference to **jealousy,** including synonyms such as **envy,** with a **J.***

DISCUSS

• What did you learn about jealousy from these scriptures? Where does it originate?

will not inherit the Kingdom of God

push

• What is true of those who practice the deeds of the flesh?

will not inherit kingdom of God

• How is the flesh to be dealt with, according to Romans 13:14?

• How is it possible for us to do so? (Hint: take another look at Titus 3:5.)

God saved us

sexual promiscuity and sensuality, not in strife and jealousy.

14 But put on the Lord Jesus Christ, and make no provision for the flesh in regard to its lusts.

TITUS 3:3–5

3 For we also once were foolish ourselves, disobedient, deceived, enslaved to various lusts and pleasures, spending our life in malice and envy, hateful, hating one another.

4 But when the kindness of God our Savior and His love for mankind appeared,

5 He saved us, not on the basis of deeds

which we have done in righteousness, but according to His mercy, by the washing of regeneration and renewing by the Holy Spirit.

INSIGHT

Jealousy and *envy* are often used as synonyms for resentment over someone else having something you wish you had. Signs of envy include feeling unhappy over the success of another and taking delight in another person's failures.

OBSERVE

As we've seen in previous lessons, each deadly distraction can lead to other sins. Let's look at some of the results of envy and jealousy.

PROVERBS 6:34

For jealousy enrages a man, and he will not spare in the day of vengeance.

Leader: *Read aloud Proverbs 6:34; James 3:13–16; and Galatians 5:25–26.*

- *Have the group say aloud and mark with a **J** each reference to **jealousy,** including synonyms such as **envying.***

JAMES 3:13–16

13 Who among you is wise and understanding? Let him show by his good behavior his

DISCUSS

• Discuss the kind of behaviors jealousy leads to.

• According to James 3:13–16, how does jealousy affect a person's thinking?

• According to Galatians 5:25–26, how does jealousy affect our relationships?

deeds in the gentleness of wisdom.

14 But if you have bitter jealousy and selfish ambition in your heart, do not be arrogant and so lie against the truth.

15 This wisdom is not that which comes down from above, but is earthly, natural, demonic.

16 For where jealousy and selfish ambition exist, there is disorder and every evil thing.

GALATIANS 5:25–26

25 If we live by the Spirit, let us also walk by the Spirit.

26 Let us not become boastful, challenging one another, envying one another.

1 SAMUEL 18:5–16

5 So David went out wherever Saul sent him, and prospered; and Saul set him over the men of war. And it was pleasing in the sight of all the people and also in the sight of Saul's servants.

6 It happened as they were coming, when David returned from killing the Philistine, that the women came out of all the cities of Israel, singing and dancing, to meet King Saul, with tambourines, with joy and with musical instruments.

7 The women sang as they played, and said, "Saul has slain his thousands, and David his ten thousands."

OBSERVE

After David's victory over Goliath, Saul brought David into the palace as commander of his army.

Leader: Read 1 Samuel 18:5–16 aloud. Have the group…
- *circle (**David**) each time his name appears.*
- *draw a box around **Saul** each time his name appears:* ☐

DISCUSS

- Discuss what you learned about David and Saul in this passage.

- Specifically, what sparked Saul's jealousy?

- What emotions did Saul display?

- How did Saul's jealousy affect his thinking?

- What effect did jealousy have on Saul and David's relationship?

8 Then Saul became very angry, for this saying displeased him; and he said, "They have ascribed to David ten thousands, but to me they have ascribed thousands. Now what more can he have but the kingdom?"

9 Saul looked at David with suspicion from that day on.

10 Now it came about on the next day that an evil spirit from God came mightily upon Saul, and he raved in the midst of the house, while David was playing the harp with his hand, as usual; and a spear was in Saul's hand.

11 Saul hurled the spear for he thought, "I will pin David to the wall." But David escaped from his presence twice.

12 Now Saul was afraid of David, for the LORD was with him but had departed from Saul.

13 Therefore Saul removed him from his presence and appointed him as his commander of a thousand; and he went out and came in before the people.

14 David was prospering in all his ways for the LORD was with him.

15 When Saul saw that he was prospering greatly, he dreaded him.

16 But all Israel and Judah loved David, and he went out and came in before them.

• What did you learn about David in verses 12–16? Did Saul's attempt to murder David keep the younger man from honoring God? Explain your answer.

• If you are the victim of another person's jealousy, what is your responsibility?

• Should another person's jealousy prompt you to stop doing what God has called you to do? Explain your answer.

OBSERVE

Acts 13:16–41 describes Paul preaching a message in Antioch. The people were so interested that they begged to hear more the following Sabbath. But as we'll read in this next passage, not everyone was pleased by his popularity.

Leader: Read Acts 13:44–46 aloud. Have the group…

* *draw a box around each reference to the* **Jews,** *including pronouns:* ☐
* *mark the word* **jealousy** *with a* **J.**

DISCUSS

* Who had assembled to hear the word of the Lord?

* What did you learn about the Jews?

* Why do you think they responded in this way?

ACTS 13:44–46

44 The next Sabbath nearly the whole city assembled to hear the word of the Lord.

45 But when the Jews saw the crowds, they were filled with jealousy and began contradicting the things spoken by Paul, and were blaspheming.

46 Paul and Barnabas spoke out boldly and said, "It was necessary that the word of God be spoken to you first; since you repudiate it and judge yourselves unworthy of eternal life, behold, we are turning to the Gentiles."

• Have you ever been upset by another person's popularity?

• Discuss ways that jealousy can distract you and keep you from going forward on your spiritual journey.

PHILIPPIANS 2:1–4

1 Therefore if there is any encouragement in Christ, if there is any consolation of love, if there is any fellowship of the Spirit, if any affection and compassion,

2 make my joy complete by being of the same mind, maintaining the same love, united in spirit, intent on one purpose.

3 Do nothing from selfishness or empty conceit, but with

OBSERVE

As believers, how can we resist the temptation to jealousy or defeat envy when it creeps into our thoughts?

Leader: Read aloud the following passages. Don't mark anything this time; simply read the verses. Then we will discuss each passage and how it relates to jealousy.

DISCUSS

• Walk though each of these scriptures individually and discuss how they relate to handling jealousy. Each passage suggests a specific antidote to envy. Discuss how each antidote would look when put to work in your life.

• What remedy did you find in Philippians 2:1–4, and how could you apply it?

humility of mind regard one another as more important than yourselves;

4 do not merely look out for your own personal interests, but also for the interests of others.

ROMANS 12:10

Be devoted to one another in brotherly love; give preference to one another in honor.

PHILIPPIANS 4:11–13

11 Not that I speak from want, for I have learned to be content in whatever circumstances I am.

12 I know how to get along with humble means, and I also know how to live in prosperity; in any and

• In Romans 12:10?

every circumstance I have learned the secret of being filled and going hungry, both of having abundance and suffering need.

13 I can do all things through Him who strengthens me.

PSALM 37:1–2, 7

1 Do not fret because of evildoers, be not envious toward wrongdoers.

2 For they will wither quickly like the grass and fade like the green herb....

7 Rest in the LORD and wait patiently for Him; do not fret because of him who prospers in his way, because of the man who carries out wicked schemes.

• In Philippians 4:11–13?

• In Psalm 37:1–2, 7?

WRAP IT UP

Jealousy, that green-eyed monster, doesn't have to be a distraction to your spiritual growth. You can learn to overcome those jealous feelings, realize your own worth in God's eyes, and appreciate others.

Learning to let go of jealous feelings is a process. We have all been tempted to envy what another person has, but if we could look at our lives from God's perspective, jealousy would lose its power. God has chosen us. He loves each of us with an everlasting love and has a plan for our lives (Jeremiah 31:3; 29:11). He tells us we are His workmanship (Ephesians 2:10) and by His grace we are what we are (1 Corinthians 15:10). God's plans for us may not unfold at the same time as His plan for another. Rather than fretting, *What about me?* our role is to be patient and wait for God, believing that He is working out His purpose in our lives for our ultimate good and His glory.

You may have noticed that each of the fatal distractions we have looked at so far—pride, anger, and jealousy—are connected. Each takes root in our lives when we focus on ourselves rather than on God, believing that joy comes from chasing after our own desires rather than pursuing His heart. In fact, choosing independence from God is the root of every sin, including those we'll look at in the next three weeks.

If you are struggling with jealousy, you have forgotten a key truth about God's character:

> *For the LORD God is a sun and shield;*
> *The LORD gives grace and glory;*
> *No good thing does He withhold from those who*
> *walk uprightly. (Psalm 84:11)*

As we bring this week's lesson to a close, examine your heart closely. Is there someone you don't like being around because you feel threatened by what God has given them? Ask God to forgive you for any jealousy or envy you may be harboring. And ask Him to help you find satisfaction in Him alone:

How blessed is the one whom You choose
and bring near to You to dwell in Your courts.
We will be satisfied with the goodness of Your house,
Your holy temple. (Psalm 65:4)

We live in a culture of self-indulgence and excess. We are bombarded daily with ads urging us to "supersize" it. If you aren't careful, that large drink you order may be the size of a small bucket. We've become so accustomed to consuming more than enough that the idea of gluttony as a sin seems archaic. Sermons on this topic are rare, and even Christians seem to believe we just can't help ourselves. But the Bible is clear that excessive eating or drinking (both alcoholic and nonalcoholic) is a signal that something is wrong in our hearts and lives. Let's see what truths we can uncover about gluttony this week.

DISCUSS

Leader: *Have the group briefly discuss their definitions of gluttony.*

OBSERVE

As with any sin, gluttony brings consequences. Let's look at the problems that accompany this fatal distraction.

Leader: *Read the following scriptures aloud.*
  • *Have the group say and double underline all references to **food** and **drink**, including **eating** and **drinking**, along with the words **gluttonous**, **glutton(s)**, and **drunkard**.*

PROVERBS 23:19–21

19 Listen, my son, and be wise, and direct your heart in the way.

20 Do not be with heavy drinkers of wine, or with gluttonous eaters of meat;

21 for the heavy drinker and the glutton will come to poverty, and drowsiness will clothe one with rags.

PROVERBS 28:7

He who keeps the law is a discerning son, but he who is a companion of gluttons humiliates his father.

PROVERBS 25:16

Have you found honey? Eat only what you need, that you not have it in excess and vomit it.

DEUTERONOMY 21:18–21

18 If any man has a stubborn and rebellious son who will not obey his father or his mother, and when they chastise him, he will not even listen to them,

19 then his father and mother shall seize him, and bring him out to the elders of his city at

INSIGHT

Gluttony can be defined as "excessive indulgence in eating and/or drinking, a strong appetite for something beyond what you need." Gluttony is a result of demanding more pleasure from something than it was made for.

The early church fathers described this deadly sin as a fixation on pleasuring the palate. The concern was not so much about overeating or drinking too much, but about an excessive focus on sensory pleasure, which undermines self-discipline and distracts our attention from God.

DISCUSS

• What did you learn from marking the references to food and drink?

• What other character issues tend to accompany gluttony?

drunkeness

selfishness

• Examine your own life. Can you identify with any of these scriptures? Why or why not?

No, I don't over eat or get drunk on a regular basis

the gateway of his hometown.

20 They shall say to the elders of his city, "This son of ours is stubborn and rebellious, he will not obey us, he is a glutton and a drunkard."

21 Then all the men of his city shall stone him to death; so you shall remove the evil from your midst, and all Israel will hear of it and fear.

Amos 6:4–7

4 Those who recline on beds of ivory and sprawl on their couches, and eat lambs from the flock and calves from the midst of the stall,

5 who improvise to the sound of the harp, and like David have composed songs for themselves,

6 who drink wine from sacrificial bowls while they anoint themselves with the finest of oils, yet they have not grieved over the ruin of Joseph.

7 Therefore, they will now go into exile at the head of the exiles, and the sprawlers' banqueting will pass away.

OBSERVE

Let's look at the attitude of gluttons.

Leader: Read Amos 6:4–7 and Isaiah 22:12–13 aloud.

- *Have the group double underline all references to **eating** and **drinking**.*

DISCUSS

- Discuss the lifestyle described in these passages.

over indulgence

- Note what the people described in Amos 6:6 were using to drink their wine. What does this reveal about their attitude?

care only about satisfying themselves

• What or who seems to be their top priority? Explain your answer.

themselves

• According to Amos 6:7, what is the consequence of their actions?

go into exile

• What does their "eat and drink, for tomorrow we may die" attitude say about their relationship to God? *They don't believe in eternity heaven — w/ God*

ISAIAH 22:12–13

12 Therefore in that day the Lord GOD of hosts called you to weeping, to wailing, to shaving the head and to wearing sackcloth.

13 Instead, there is gaiety and gladness, killing of cattle and slaughtering of sheep, eating of meat and drinking of wine: "Let us eat and drink, for tomorrow we may die."

INSIGHT

Rather than heed the prophets' warnings of judgment, the leaders of both Israel and Judah were distracted from pursuing righteousness by their overindulgence.

ISAIAH 5:11–12, 22–23

11 Woe to those who rise early in the morning that they may pursue strong drink, who stay up late in the evening that wine may inflame them!

12 Their banquets are accompanied by lyre and harp, by tambourine and flute, and by wine; but they do not pay attention to the deeds of the LORD, nor do they consider the work of His hands....

22 Woe to those who are heroes in drinking wine and valiant men in mixing strong drink,

23 who justify the wicked for a bribe, and

OBSERVE

Apparently, heavy consumption of wine was prevalent in Isaiah's day. It is mentioned in two of the six "woes," as certain prophecies of judgment are known.

Leader: Read Isaiah 5:11–12, 22–23 aloud. Have the group...

- *circle each occurrence of the word* **woe.**
- *double underline all references to* **eating** *and* **drinking.**

DISCUSS

- Who are these woes directed to, and what did you learn about these people?

- According to verse 12, what are they distracted from?

• How does this relate to what we have seen so far about gluttony?

• Discuss where you see examples of heroes in drinking in our culture today. How is their behavior generally viewed?

OBSERVE

The apostle Paul wrote to the believers in Corinth about the proper perspective in regard to eating.

Leader: Read 1 Corinthians 6:12–13 and 19–20 aloud. Have the group…
  • *circle each pronoun referring to **Paul** and to **believers: me, I, you.***
  • *double underline all references to **food.***

DISCUSS

• What did you learn from marking the references to believers?

not about us

take away the rights of the ones who are in the right!

1 CORINTHIANS 6:12–13, 19–20

12 All things are lawful for me, but not all things are profitable. All things are lawful for me, but I will not be mastered by anything.

13 Food is for the stomach and the stomach is for food, but God will do away with both of them. Yet the body is not for immorality, but for the

Lord, and the Lord is for the body....

19 Or do you not know that your body is a temple of the Holy Spirit who is in you, whom you have from God, and that you are not your own?

20 For you have been bought with a price: therefore glorify God in your body.

• Discuss how this relates to our study on gluttony.

• What does it mean to "glorify God in your body"?

GENESIS 25:29–34

29 When Jacob had cooked stew, Esau came in from the field and he was famished;

30 and Esau said to Jacob, "Please let me have a swallow of that red stuff there, for I am famished."

OBSERVE

Esau, the oldest son of Isaac, was a rugged, strong-willed hunter who preferred the outdoors and was his father's favorite son.

Leader: Read Genesis 25:29–34 and Hebrews 12:16–17 aloud. Have the group...
- *mark each reference to Esau, including pronouns, with an* **E.**
- *double underline all references to **food.***

DISCUSS

• What did you learn about Esau in the Genesis passage?

INSIGHT

The word *despised* means "counted as worthless or as having little or no value."

• What did Esau value, and what did he despise?   *food*
birthright

• What dictated the choices Esau made?
hunger

• What did the writer of Hebrews have to say about Esau?

Therefore his name was called Edom.

31 But Jacob said, "First sell me your birthright."

32 Esau said, "Behold, I am about to die; so of what use then is the birthright to me?"

33 And Jacob said, "First swear to me"; so he swore to him, and sold his birthright to Jacob.

34 Then Jacob gave Esau bread and lentil stew; and he ate and drank, and rose and went on his way. Thus Esau despised his birthright.

HEBREWS 12:16–17

16 [See to it] that there be no immoral or godless person like

Esau, who sold his own birthright for a single meal.

17 For you know that even afterwards, when he desired to inherit the blessing, he was rejected, for he found no place for repentance, though he sought for it with tears.

---

1 SAMUEL 2:12–17

12 Now the sons of Eli were worthless men; they did not know the LORD

13 and the custom of the priests with the people. When any man was offering a sacrifice, the priest's servant would come while the meat was boiling, with

• Do you see any similarities between your behavior and that of Esau? Does the desire for food or drink ever dictate important choices in your life?

OBSERVE

Eli's sons were the most prominent priests at Shiloh. But what was the most prominent concern in their lives?

Leader: Read 1 Samuel 2:12–17 aloud. Have the group say and...
- *draw a box around each reference to* **Eli's sons,** *including* **priest(s)** *and* **young men:**
- *double underline every mention of* **meat.**

INSIGHT

The law mandated that the fat of the sacrificial animal was to be burned on the altar to the Lord (Leviticus 7:31). It also specified which portions were to be given to the priests (Deuteronomy 18:3).

DISCUSS

• Discuss what you learned about Eli's sons.

selfish & greedy.

• According to verse 17, what made the sin of the young men so great before the Lord? What did they value? What did they despise?

• So you don't miss it, what dictated their behavior?

gluttony

a three-pronged fork in his hand.

14 Then he would thrust it into the pan, or kettle, or caldron, or pot; all that the fork brought up the priest would take for himself. Thus they did in Shiloh to all the Israelites who came there.

15 Also, before they burned the fat, the priest's servant would come and say to the man who was sacrificing, "Give the priest meat for roasting, as he will not take boiled meat from you, only raw."

16 If the man said to him, "They must surely burn the fat first, and then take as much as you desire," then he

would say, "No, but you shall give it to me now; and if not, I will take it by force."

¹⁷ Thus the sin of the young men was very great before the LORD, for the men despised the offering of the LORD.

• In light of what you've seen in the life of Esau and the sons of Eli, discuss how gluttony distracts a person from spiritual growth.

• Is there excess in your life? Are you eating, drinking, and desiring more than you really need? If so, what is the result?

ROMANS 13:13–14

¹³ Let us behave properly as in the day, not in carousing and drunkenness, not in sexual promiscuity and sensuality, not in strife and jealousy.

¹⁴ But put on the Lord Jesus Christ, and make no provision for the flesh in regard to its lusts.

OBSERVE ✝

In several of his letters to the early church, the apostle Paul reminded believers how to behave in ways that demonstrated their love and devotion to Christ.

Leader: Read Romans 13:13–14 and Galatians 5:19–21 aloud. Have the group...
   • *double underline each reference to* **drunkenness.**
   • *draw a box around each reference to* **the flesh.**

DISCUSS

- In calling believers to proper behavior, Paul specifically identified improper behavior. What did he caution them to avoid?

- What did you learn from marking references to the flesh?

- What did you learn about drunkenness? What place does it have in the life of a believer? *No place*

- How does that relate to what you've learned about gluttony? *overeating*

GALATIANS 5:19–21

19 Now the deeds of the flesh are evident, which are: immorality, impurity, sensuality,

20 idolatry, sorcery, enmities, strife, jealousy, outbursts of anger, disputes, dissensions, factions,

21 envying, drunkenness, carousing, and things like these, of which I forewarn you, just as I have forewarned you, that those who practice such things will not inherit the kingdom of God.

GALATIANS 5:22–24

22 But the fruit of the Spirit is love, joy, peace, patience, kindness, goodness, faithfulness,

23 gentleness, self-control; against such things there is no law.

24 Now those who belong to Christ Jesus have crucified the flesh with its passions and desires.

1 PETER 4:1–4

1 Therefore, since Christ has suffered in the flesh, arm yourselves also with the same purpose, because he who has suffered in the flesh has ceased from sin,

2 so as to live the rest of the time in the

OBSERVE

God does not leave us on our own in the battle against gluttony.

Leader: Read Galatians 5:22–24 and 1 Peter 4:1–4 aloud. Have the group…

- *circle each reference to **believers**, including the phrase **those who belong to Christ** and the pronouns **yourselves** and **you**.*
- *double underline all references to **drunkenness** and **drinking**.*

DISCUSS

- Discuss how a believer can overcome gluttony—drinking and/or eating in excess—based on what you read in these passages.

- What are some practical ways to apply the truths you have seen to your own life?

  own bodies are God's temple

• How are we to view the flesh and its desires?

• According to 1 Peter 4:1–2, how are believers to live, and why? What is the guiding motivation of our lives?

Christ suffered in the flesh

• What does 1 Peter 4:4 warn you to expect from old drinking or partying buddies or from overeating friends?

• Discuss some practical ways to respond to them.

flesh no longer for the lusts of men, but for the will of God.

3 For the time already past is sufficient for you to have carried out the desire of the Gentiles, having pursued a course of sensuality, lusts, drunkenness, carousing, drinking parties and abominable idolatries.

4 In all this, they are surprised that you do not run with them into the same excesses of dissipation, and they malign you.

ECCLESIASTES 10:16–17

16 Woe to you, O land, whose king is a lad and whose princes feast in the morning.

17 Blessed are you, O land, whose king is of nobility and whose princes eat at the appropriate time—for strength and not for drunkenness.

PROVERBS 30:8–9

8 Keep deception and lies far from me, give me neither poverty nor riches; feed me with the food that is my portion,

9 That I not be full and deny You and say, "Who is the LORD?" Or that I not be in want and steal, and profane the name of my God.

OBSERVE

Leader: *Read Ecclesiastes 10:16–17 and Proverbs 30:8–9 aloud.*

- *Have the group say aloud and double underline all references to **eating** and **drinking**.*

DISCUSS

- Discuss the contrasts being made in each of these passages.

- As we bring this week's topic to a close, let's consider how these verses apply to you personally. You may not be a king, but if you are a Christian, your life is an example others will follow. What did you learn from these verses about the leader who has his appetites under control? Which leader do you look like?

WRAP IT UP

As we have seen, gluttony is an umbrella term that includes overeating, drinking too much, or an excessive focus on foods or drinks. Gluttony is much more than simply being overweight. A thin person can be a glutton. Your heart attitude determines whether you've placed too high a priority on the "pleasures of the palate."

Focusing on food can affect you physically. It may result in illness, cause lethargy, dull your senses, and even reduce your mental capacities, making you unable to make wise choices. Overindulging in alcoholic beverages will impact your relationships, emotions, inhibitions, and reasoning ability. Most important, a misplaced priority on food or drink of any kind can affect you spiritually and even be fatal to your spiritual growth. When you look to anything other than God as your source of satisfaction, you will inevitably be disappointed. And as others witness your choices, what will they conclude about the value you place on your relationship with God?

Enjoying food and drink is not a sin. God gave us these gifts for our pleasure. However, when that pleasure turns into excess or we turn to it for comfort instead of seeking God, then we are in trouble.

So how do we avoid or overcome gluttony? We practice self-control, which is part of the fruit of the Spirit (Galatians 5:22–23). Self-control, or self-discipline, means controlling the desires of the flesh rather than allowing them mastery over us. But this can't be done apart from the power of the Holy Spirit within us.

This week ask yourself this question: *What do I hunger and thirst for above all else?* If the answer is anything other than God and His Word, you need to seek His help in breaking the grip your appetite has on your life.

You probably know someone who is lazy, who never seems to get anywhere professionally or personally. In every group of people there seems to be at least one individual who takes but doesn't contribute; this person is first in line for a handout, last to volunteer for any tasks. This sort of laziness, or sloth, seems obvious to the rest of us.

But what about more subtle ways this sin inches into our lives? Maybe we execute our responsibilities in a sloppy manner, or we look away when we see a need because we don't want to sacrifice our leisure time. In most churches, it is said that 20 percent of the people do 80 percent of the work. If that's true, what does that reveal about the priorities of the rest of the people? What about you? Are you in danger of being distracted from God's best for you, of losing your sense of purpose and motivation because of slothfulness?

DISCUSS

Leader: Open by having group members explain how they recognize slothfulness or laziness in a person, as well as some ways we see a slothful attitude demonstrated in our culture today.

OBSERVE

Leader: Read aloud the following verses from Proverbs.

- *Have the group say aloud and draw a box around each reference to **the lazy person,** including pronouns as well as synonyms such as **sluggard** and **idle.***

PROVERBS 6:6–11

⁶ Go to the ant, O sluggard, observe her ways and be wise,

⁷ which, having no chief, officer or ruler,

8 prepares her food in the summer and gathers her provision in the harvest.

9 How long will you lie down, O sluggard? When will you arise from your sleep?

10 "A little sleep, a little slumber, a little folding of the hands to rest"—

11 your poverty will come in like a vagabond and your need like an armed man.

PROVERBS 13:4

The soul of the sluggard craves and gets nothing, but the soul of the diligent is made fat.

PROVERBS 15:19

The way of the lazy is as a hedge of thorns, but the path of the upright is a highway.

INSIGHT

Slothfulness is often characterized by laziness, an unwillingness to work, a lack of self-discipline. Slothfulness is the sin of doing nothing— or as little as possible.

DISCUSS

• Discuss the contrasts being made in several of these scriptures.

• What are the results of laziness as identified in these verses?

PROVERBS 19:15

Laziness casts into a deep sleep, and an idle man will suffer hunger.

PROVERBS 20:4

The sluggard does not plow after the autumn, so he begs during the harvest and has nothing.

• What characterizes a life of diligent service?

PROVERBS 21:25–26

25 The desire of the sluggard puts him to death, for his hands refuse to work;

26 all day long he is craving, while the righteous gives and does not hold back.

PROVERBS 26:14–16

14 As the door turns on its hinges, so does the sluggard on his bed.

15 The sluggard buries his hand in the dish; he is weary of bringing it to his mouth again.

16 The sluggard is wiser in his own eyes than seven men who can give a discreet answer.

2 THESSALONIANS 3:6–11

6 Now we command you, brethren, in the name of our Lord Jesus Christ, that you keep away from every brother who leads an unruly life and not according to the tradition which you received from us.

7 For you yourselves know how you ought to follow our example, because we did not act in an undisciplined manner among you,

OBSERVE

Let's jump from Proverbs into the New Testament. In Thessalonica, Greece, many in the local church were not working. Instead, they expected the church to take care of them. The apostle Paul wrote to the believers in that city, on behalf of himself, Silvanus, and Timothy, warning about the dangers of idleness.

Leader: Read 2 Thessalonians 3:6–11 aloud. Have the group…

- *circle each reference to **the Thessalonian believers,** including the word **brethren** and the pronoun **you.***
- *draw a squiggly line like this* 〰️ *under each **we** and **us** referring to **Paul, Sylvanus, and Timothy.***

DISCUSS

- What did Paul command the Thessalonians to do? have self-discipline

• What authority did he have to do so?

From God

• What did you learn about Paul, Silvanus, and Timothy? What behavior did they model for others to follow?

productive + display workmanship, serve as a model

• Discuss what you learned about those Thessalonian believers who did not follow this example. What impact did their actions have on others?

Burden to others

8 nor did we eat anyone's bread without paying for it, but with labor and hardship we kept working night and day so that we would not be a burden to any of you;

9 not because we do not have the right to this, but in order to offer ourselves as a model for you, so that you would follow our example.

10 For even when we were with you, we used to give you this order: if anyone is not willing to work, then he is not to eat, either.

11 For we hear that some among you are leading an undisciplined life, doing no work at all, but acting like busybodies.

LUKE 19:20–26

20 Another [slave] came, saying, "Master, here is your mina, which I kept put away in a handkerchief;

21 for I was afraid of you, because you are an exacting man; you take up what you did not lay down and reap what you did not sow."

22 He said to him, "By your own words I will judge you, you worthless slave. Did you know that I am an exacting man, taking up what I did not lay down and reaping what I did not sow?

23 "Then why did you not put my money in the bank,

OBSERVE

Jesus told a parable to correct the mistaken belief that God's kingdom would appear immediately. The story explained what Christ expects of His followers while He is gone.

In the parable a nobleman gave one mina, or coin, to each of ten servants and instructed them to "do business until I come back." When he returned, the servants came to report what they had done. The first two invested well. Let's read the account of the third servant.

Leader: Read Luke 19:20–26 aloud. Have the group…

- *mark every reference to **money**, including pronouns, with a dollar sign, like this: $*
- *draw a box around each reference to **the slave**, including pronouns.*

INSIGHT

A *mina* was equal to approximately one hundred days' worth of wages for a laborer.

DISCUSS

- What did you learn about this slave? What did his master call him? *worthless*

  → *afraid of his master*

- What was the slave accountable to do, according to verse 23? *invest it*

- Why did the nobleman take this slave's mina and give it to the one who had ten already? *more shall be given to you*

- What did you learn about the nobleman's expectations, and what does that have to do with slothfulness? *make an effort to invest*

- Discuss the ways in which laziness, or sloth, becomes a trap for believers.

and having come, I would have collected it with interest?"

24 Then he said to the bystanders, "Take the mina away from him and give it to the one who has the ten minas."

25 And they said to him, "Master, he has ten minas already."

26 I tell you that to everyone who has, more shall be given, but from the one who does not have, even what he does have shall be taken away.

PROVERBS 10:4–5

⁴ Poor is he who works with a negligent hand, but the hand of the diligent makes rich.

⁵ He who gathers in summer is a son who acts wisely, but he who sleeps in harvest is a son who acts shamefully.

PROVERBS 22:29

Do you see a man skilled in his work? He will stand before kings; he will not stand before obscure men.

PROVERBS 12:11, 24

¹¹ He who tills his land will have plenty of bread, but he who pursues worthless things lacks sense....

OBSERVE

You have a choice to make about how you will use your time and abilities. Each option brings consequences, either negative or positive.

Leader: Read aloud the following verses from Proverbs and Ecclesiastes 11:4. Have the group...
- *draw a box around each reference to* **slothfulness,** *including pronouns and synonyms like* **negligent** *and* **slack.**
- *circle each reference to* **the diligent person** *or* **skilled man.**

DISCUSS

- What did you learn about the slothful individual? What does this behavior look like?

- What did you learn about those who are hard working? What behaviors mark their lives? *They will stand before kings plenty of food*

• From what you have seen, what motivation do we have to work hard?

will have plenty

• Discuss the respective consequences of sloth and diligence. *not get anything*

• How would you describe your own work ethic? Explain your answer.

• What, if anything, do you need to do to overcome slothfulness in your own life?

24 The hand of the diligent will rule, but the slack hand will be put to forced labor.

PROVERBS 28:19

He who tills his land will have plenty of food, but he who follows empty pursuits will have poverty in plenty.

PROVERBS 31:27

She looks well to the ways of her household, and does not eat the bread of idleness.

ECCLESIASTES 11:4

He who watches the wind will not sow and he who looks at the clouds will not reap.

EXODUS 20:9–11

9 Six days you shall labor and do all your work,

10 but the seventh day is a sabbath of the LORD your God; in it you shall not do any work, you or your son or your daughter, your male or your female servant or your cattle or your sojourner who stays with you.

11 For in six days the LORD made the heavens and the earth, the sea and all that is in them, and rested on the seventh day; therefore the LORD blessed the sabbath day and made it holy.

2 THESSALONIANS 3:10–12, 14–15

10 For even when we were with you, we

OBSERVE

Work is one of the basic principles of a believer's conduct. As far back as Exodus, it has been part of God's plan for His people. It comes with many benefits.

Leader: Read Exodus 20:9–11 and 2 Thessalonians 3:10–12, 14–15 aloud.
- *Have the group say aloud and underline each reference to **labor** or **work.***

DISCUSS

- What did you learn from these scriptures about working? What are some benefits and purposes of working?

you git to eat

• What consequence is there for any able bodied persons who are unwilling to work and provide for themselves?

no one would associate with them, put to shame

• What is our responsibility toward them?

to help, encourage them to be productive

used to give you this order: if anyone is not willing to work, then he is not to eat, either.

11 For we hear that some among you are leading an undisciplined life, doing no work at all, but acting like busybodies.

12 Now such persons we command and exhort in the Lord Jesus Christ to work in quiet fashion and eat their own bread....

14 If anyone does not obey our instruction in this letter, take special note of that person and do not associate with him, so that he will be put to shame.

15 Yet do not regard him as an enemy, but admonish him as a brother.

COLOSSIANS 3:22–24

22 Slaves, in all things obey those who are your masters on earth, not with external service, as those who merely please men, but with sincerity of heart, fearing the Lord.

23 Whatever you do, do your work heartily, as for the Lord rather than for men,

24 knowing that from the Lord you will receive the reward of the inheritance. It is the Lord Christ whom you serve.

OBSERVE

Before we close this week's study, let's look at two more verses. In addition to everything we have seen so far, what other reasons do we have to work hard? In this passage *slaves* could be translated *servants*. In our context this passage would apply to an employer/employee relationship.

Leader: Read Colossians 3:22–24 aloud.

> • *Have the group say aloud and underline each occurrence of the words **service**, **work**, and **serve**.*

DISCUSS

• What commands did you find in these verses? obey masters, do work heartily

• What motive is given for obeying these commands? inheritance

• Just to be sure you don't miss it, who are we working for? the Lord

WRAP IT UP

Sluggards, also described in Scripture as the slothful, aim to do as little as possible and to live off the labor of others. Like the animal that gives rise to the name, the person of sloth is slow moving, not concerned about completing tasks quickly or well. Lazy people want a life of ease with no commitment or responsibility. Sloth results in all kinds of problems. These may include loss of job, fractured relationships, stress, poverty, and an acute focus on self instead of pleasing God.

But the signs of sloth are not always obvious. A spirit of laziness can creep into our lives when we find excuses for not reading and studying scripture or when we can't seem to find time to participate in the work of the local church or when we're just too tired to pray. Spiritual laziness leads to compromise and spiritual ignorance, which will keep you from maturing in the things of the Lord.

Sloth is a tool of the enemy. He knows that if you allow laziness to rule, you will never fully realize the hope and promises that are yours in Jesus Christ. The good news is that laziness doesn't have to become a fatal distraction. You can make a choice to turn away from that sin, to view every task as an opportunity to faithfully serve the Lord.

Spend some time in prayer this week, asking God to show you any areas of laziness in your life. Consider the following questions:

- *Do I expect others to do what I can do, to provide what I need?*
- *Am I a giver or a taker?*
- *Is there any area in my spiritual life where laziness has taken over? Is it prayer? Reading my Bible? Is it ministry? What steps can I take to make a change?*

• *Besides my spiritual life, is there any area of my life where laziness has slipped in?*

Remember, you are accountable for the talents and spiritual gifts God has given you. You are meant to be "a vessel for honor, sanctified, useful to the Master, prepared for every good work" (2 Timothy 2:21). Don't waste the opportunities of today.

Cameron - a little warae
Devin - runny nose

We live in a culture set on accumulating more of anything and everything, so much so that some people rent storage units to hold it all. Many are obsessed with having the latest gadget, while others are preoccupied with building the biggest investment portfolio. This week we'll look at the consequences of *greed,* our sixth and final fatal distraction.

DISCUSS

Leader: Guide the group in discussing various ways that greed seems to be rampant in today's culture.

OBSERVE

In the opening words of his letter to the Romans, the apostle Paul described those who choose to worship items in creation rather than the Creator Himself.

Leader: Read Romans 1:28–32 aloud. Have the group…
- *mark a slash like this ╱ through each occurrence of **they** and **them,** which in this passage refers to **unbelievers.***
- *draw a box around each reference to **greed,** including synonyms.*

ROMANS 1:28–32

28 And just as they did not see fit to acknowledge God any longer, God gave them over to a depraved mind, to do those things which are not proper,

29 being filled with all unrighteousness, wickedness, greed, evil; full of envy, murder, strife, deceit, malice; they are gossips,

30 slanderers, haters of God, insolent, arrogant, boastful, inventors of evil, disobedient to parents,

31 without under-
standing, untrust-
worthy, unloving,
unmerciful;

32 and although they
know the ordinance of
God, that those who
practice such things
are worthy of death,
they not only do the
same, but also give
hearty approval to
those who practice
them.

INSIGHT

Greed is "an excessive desire to
acquire or possess more than one
needs." Greed is not limited to a fixation on material wealth, but could
also include the pursuit of power and
position.

DISCUSS

• From what you just read, how does God
describe an unbeliever, the one with a
depraved mind? *do improper things*

• How does what you saw relate to greed?
to get what you want you do wicked things

• What three words did you find surround-
ing greed in verse 29? What does this
indicate about the seriousness of this sin?
unrighteousness wicked, evil

• According to verse 32, what is the penalty
for greed and other wickedness?
worthy of death

• Should the behaviors described in these
verses be a normal practice in the life of a
believer? Explain your answer.

no

OBSERVE

In a world obsessed with more and bigger, what is the proper perspective for a believer?

Leader: *Read the following verses aloud.*
- *Have the group draw a box around each reference to **greed**, including synonyms such as **lust.***

DISCUSS

- What did you learn about greed from these passages? What does it amount to, according to Colossians 3:5?

  greed should not be present

  idolatry

- In what ways could greed be considered idolatry? *Consumes you worshipping those things*

EPHESIANS 5:3

But immorality or any impurity or greed must not even be named among you, as is proper among saints.

COLOSSIANS 3:5–6

5 Therefore consider the members of your earthly body as dead to immorality, impurity, passion, evil desire, and greed, which amounts to idolatry.

6 For it is because of these things that the wrath of God will come upon the sons of disobedience.

1 JOHN 2:15–17

15 Do not love the world nor the things in the world. If anyone loves the world, the

love of the Father is
not in him.

16 For all that is in
the world, the lust of
the flesh and the lust
of the eyes and the
boastful pride of life, is
not from the Father,
but is from the world.

17 The world is pass-
ing away, and also its
lusts; but the one who
does the will of God
lives forever.

PROVERBS 23:4–5

4 Do not weary
yourself to gain wealth,
cease from your consid-
eration of it.

5 When you set your
eyes on it, it is gone.
For wealth certainly
makes itself wings like
an eagle that flies
toward the heavens.

• According to 1 John 2:16, what is the
source of lust (a synonym for greed)?

worldly / earthly thing

• What do 1 John 2:17 and Proverbs 23:5
reveal about the ultimate result of pursuing more? *temporary*
passes away
empty, gone quickly

• How would greed serve as a fatal distraction, destroying a believer's spiritual
growth?

when you focus on
unnecessary things
cannot focus on
normal

OBSERVE

How does greed affect a person's attitude and behavior toward God and toward others?

Leader: Read the following verses aloud.
- *Have the group say and underline **each action of those who are greedy.***

DISCUSS

- What did you learn about the greedy person?

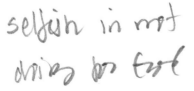
scheme

- What effect does greed have on one's relationships with others? With God?

selfish in not
doing to God

PSALM 10:3

For the wicked boasts of his heart's desire, and the greedy man curses and spurns the LORD.

PROVERBS 22:16

He who oppresses the poor to make more for himself or who gives to the rich, will only come to poverty.

MICAH 2:1–2

1 Woe to those who scheme iniquity, who work out evil on their beds! When morning comes, they do it, for it is in the power of their hands.

2 They covet fields and then seize them, and houses, and take them away. They rob a man and his house, a man and his inheritance.

ECCLESIASTES 4:7–8

7 Then I looked again at vanity under the sun.

8 There was a certain man without a dependent, having neither a son nor a brother, yet there was no end to all his labor. Indeed, his eyes were not satisfied with riches and he never asked, "And for whom am I laboring and depriving myself of pleasure?" This too is vanity and it is a grievous task.

ECCLESIASTES 5:10–11

10 He who loves money will not be satisfied with money, nor he who loves abundance with its income. This too is vanity.

OBSERVE

King Solomon had a reputation for wisdom. In fact, he wrote much of what you find in the book of Proverbs. He also may have been the author of Ecclesiastes, which offers additional insights into the results of greed.

Leader: Read Ecclesiastes 4:7–8 and 5:10–11 aloud. Have the group…
- *mark every occurrence of **vanity** with a **V**.*
- *draw a dollar sign over each reference to **riches** and **money**, like this: **$***

INSIGHT

In this context, *vanity* means "of no value" or "empty, senseless, transitory." It carries the idea that you can't take it with you.

DISCUSS

- In these passages, what attitude is described as vanity?

unsatisfied

wanting more

• Describe a situation when you have seen this prove true, either in your own life or that of others.

11 When good things increase, those who consume them increase. So what is the advantage to their owners except to look on?

OBSERVE

Jesus warned His followers about the dangers of greed.

Leader: Read aloud the following verses from Matthew, in which Jesus is speaking.

• *Have the group draw a dollar sign over each reference to* **treasure(s)** *and* **wealth.**

MATTHEW 13:22

And the one on whom seed was sown among the thorns, this is the man who hears the word, and the worry of the world and the deceitfulness of wealth choke the word, and it becomes unfruitful.

DISCUSS

• How is wealth described and what does it do, according to Matthew 13:22?

Can not serve God

MATTHEW 16:24–26

24 Then Jesus said to His disciples, "If anyone wishes to come after Me, he must deny himself, and take up his cross and follow Me.

25 "For whoever wishes to save his life will lose it; but whoever loses his life for My sake will find it.

26 "For what will it profit a man if he gains the whole world and forfeits his soul? Or what will a man give in exchange for his soul?"

MATTHEW 6:19–21, 24

19 Do not store up for yourselves treasures on earth, where moth and rust destroy, and where thieves break in and steal.

20 But store up for yourselves treasures in heaven, where neither moth nor rust destroys, and where thieves do not break in or steal;

• What connection did Jesus make between treasure and the heart?

where you heart is what you do

• What would be the end result of a life focused on gaining wealth?

meaningless
forfeits your soul

• According to Matthew 6:24, how serious is this issue to the Lord?

Cannot serve God + wealth

• What does your attitude about money reveal about you?

21 for where your treasure is, there your heart will be also....

24 No one can serve two masters; for either he will hate the one and love the other, or he will be devoted to one and despise the other. You cannot serve God and wealth.

OBSERVE

In the following passage Jesus underscored His warning against all kinds of greed by telling a parable.

Leader: *Read Luke 12:15–21 aloud. Have the group say and...*
- *draw a box around the word* **greed.**
- *underline each reference to* **the rich man,** *including pronouns.*

LUKE 12:15–21

15 Then He said to them, "Beware, and be on your guard against every form of greed; for not even when one has an abundance does his life consist of his possessions."

16 And He told them a parable, saying, "The

land of a rich man was very productive.

17 "And he began reasoning to himself, saying, 'What shall I do, since I have no place to store my crops?'

18 "Then he said, 'This is what I will do: I will tear down my barns and build larger ones, and there I will store all my grain and my goods.

19 'And I will say to my soul, "Soul, you have many goods laid up for many years to come; take your ease, eat, drink and be merry." '

20 "But God said to him, 'You fool! This very night your soul is required of you; and now who will own what you have prepared?'

DISCUSS

• Parables have one central theme. What point was Jesus making in this parable?

• What lesson from this parable can be applied to your own life?

OBSERVE

What is the proper attitude of a believer toward money, power, and possessions? Paul addressed this question in both of his letters to Timothy, a younger man the apostle was mentoring.

Leader: Read 1 Timothy 6:6–11 aloud. Have the group…
  • *circle every occurrence of (we,) which in this passage refers to **believers**.*
  • *draw a dollar sign over each reference to **wealth**, including synonyms such as **rich**.*

DISCUSS

• As believers, what should be our attitude toward wealth or money?

---

21 "So is the man who stores up treasure for himself, and is not rich toward God."

1 TIMOTHY 6:6–11

6 But godliness actually is a means of great gain when accompanied by contentment.

7 For we have brought nothing into the world, so we cannot take anything out of it either.

8 If we have food and covering, with these we shall be content.

9 But those who want to get rich fall into temptation and a snare and many foolish and harmful desires which plunge men into ruin and destruction.

10 For the love of money is a root of all sorts of evil, and some by longing for it have wandered away from the faith and pierced themselves with many griefs.

11 But flee from these things, you man of God, and pursue righteousness, godliness, faith, love, perseverance and gentleness.

• What specific dangers accompany a love of wealth or money? Explain your answer.

• According to verse 10, what exactly is the root of all sorts of evil? (Be careful as you answer this; the verse is often misquoted.) How does this relate to greed?

OBSERVE

We've seen that greed poses significant dangers. Now let's look at how we can avoid this pitfall—or escape if we've been lured into the trap.

Leader: *Read aloud Romans 13:9; Hebrews 13:5; and Colossians 3:2. Have the group...*

- *circle every occurrence of **you** and **your** that refers to **believers**.*
- *draw a box around each reference to **greed**, including the word **covet** and the phrase **love of money**.*

DISCUSS

- According to Romans 13:9, what is the principal command for believers to follow?

you shall ♥ your neighbor as yourself

- Practically speaking, what are some ways you could fulfill this command? How would this counteract greed?

concentrate on putting others first

ROMANS 13:9

For this, "You shall not commit adultery, You shall not murder, You shall not steal, You shall not covet," and if there is any other commandment, it is summed up in this saying, "You shall love your neighbor as yourself."

HEBREWS 13:5

Make sure that your character is free from the love of money, being content with what you have; for He Himself has said, "I will never desert you, nor will I ever forsake you."

COLOSSIANS 3:2

Set your mind on the things above, not on the things that are on earth.

• How can we be free from the love of money, according to Hebrews 13:5?

be content w/ what you have

• What should we be content with? On what promise does our contentment rest?

content w/ what we have + God will not desert us

• What practical step can we take to address the problem of greed, according to Colossians 3:2?

set mind on things above.

• What does it mean to set your mind on things above? How would this look in the life of a believer?

not to be materialistic be in the word

OBSERVE

Paul shared with the early church his secret for resisting the pull of greed.

Leader: *Read Philippians 4:11–12 aloud.*

- *Have the group say and circle every occurrence of the pronoun* ***I****, which here refers to* ***Paul.***

DISCUSS

- What enabled Paul to successfully overcome greed? be humble

- How could you put this secret to work in your life?

make conscious effort

PHILIPPIANS 4:11–12

11 Not that I speak from want, for I have learned to be content in whatever circumstances I am.

12 I know how to get along with humble means, and I also know how to live in prosperity; in any and every circumstance I have learned the secret of being filled and going hungry, both of having abundance and suffering need.

2 Corinthians 9:6–11

6 Now this I say, he who sows sparingly will also reap sparingly, and he who sows bountifully will also reap bountifully.

7 Each one must do just as he has purposed in his heart, not grudgingly or under compulsion, for God loves a cheerful giver.

8 And God is able to make all grace abound to you, so that always having all sufficiency in everything, you may have an abundance for every good deed;

9 as it is written, "He scattered abroad, He gave to the poor, His righteousness endures forever."

OBSERVE

Let's look at one last passage; it may be the most practical one for dealing with greed.

Leader: Read 2 Corinthians 9:6–11 aloud. Have the group…
- *double underline each reference to sow-ing and giving.*
- *mark every reference to God, including pronouns, with a triangle:* △

DISCUSS

- Discuss what you learned about giving and how it relates to greed.

  more you give

- What did you learn about God in regards to giving in this passage?

  God loves a cheerful giver.

• How does He want us to approach giving?

cheerfully

• What will He do for those who have this attitude?

will enriched in

everything

abundance for

every good deed

10 Now He who supplies seed to the <u>sower</u> and bread for food will supply and multiply your seed for <u>sowing</u> and increase the harvest of your righteousness;

11 you will be enriched in everything for all liberality, which through us is producing thanksgiving to <u>God</u>.

WRAP IT UP

Greed—a form of selfishness—is a serious problem in our society today. Greed is at the root of disgraceful corporate scandals, outrageous salaries for corporate executives of failing companies, and financial scams that have robbed countless individuals of their homes and life savings. Greed—and the resulting workaholism—is responsible for straining many marriages past the breaking point.

But greed does not affect only the world; it affects the church as well. Often greed feeds the campaigns for bigger buildings, programs, and performances, all of which can overshadow the needs of the sick, the poor, and the hurting. This phenomenon is found in both large and small churches. Sometimes a group of people within a church becomes focused on guarding all of their own "stuff," keeping it for themselves rather than sharing with others. Even where the leadership has a right perspective on money, churches and ministries are struggling because so many individuals resist the idea of giving their hard-earned money to the work of the Lord.

We have seen that God has a lot to say about greed. He has issued warnings throughout the Bible to protect us from falling into the trap of selfishness. Make no mistake: having a lot of money is not a sin. Nor is poverty a virtue. God's main concern is that greed—pursuit of more or hoarding what we have, whether little or much—will lead our hearts astray from Him. Greed amounts to idolatry, the worship of the gods of money, power, or position (Colossians 3:5).

What is the cure for greed? Giving and learning to be content (Philippians 4:11). Generous giving is the opposite of greed. Paul encouraged the Corinthians not to be selfish but to give (2 Corinthians 9). Whatever we have is to be used for the benefit of others (2 Corinthians 8:14). Christians should be the most generous people on the planet. We serve a generous God who has given to us in great abundance and who has promised to meet our every need.

As our study comes to a close, here are some ideas for how you can choose giving over greed:

- Ask God to show you if greed has crept into your life. If He does, determine today to do whatever it takes to destroy greed before it destroys your spiritual journey by turning your heart away from God.
- Next time you go shopping, ask yourself, "Do I really need this?"
- When you review your investment portfolio, bank account, or checkbook, remind yourself that—whether the balance is small or large—it is all God's money, given to you out of His goodness and blessing.
- Ask God to show you some practical ways to sow generously and then give cheerfully, joyfully.

Remember, giving is not a chore. It is a privilege to give out of your God-given abundance! Start today!

40 MINUTE BIBLE STUDIES

No-Homework
That Help Yo

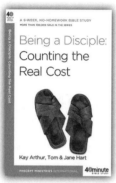

A 6-WEEK, NO-HOMEWORK BIBLE STUDY
MORE THAN 700,000 SOLD IN THE SERIES

Being a Disciple:
Counting the
Real Cost

Kay Arthur, Tom & Jane Hart

PRECEPT MINISTRIES INTERNATIONAL 40minute BIBLE STUDY

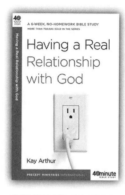

A 6-WEEK, NO-HOMEWORK BIBLE STUDY
MORE THAN 700,000 SOLD IN THE SERIES

Having a Real
Relationship
with God

Kay Arthur

PRECEPT MINISTRIES INTERNATIONAL 40minute BIBLE STUDY

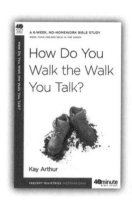

A 6-WEEK, NO-HOMEWORK BIBLE STUDY
MORE THAN 700,000 SOLD IN THE SERIES

How Do You
Walk the Walk
You Talk?

Kay Arthur

PRECEPT MINISTRIES INTERNATIONAL 40minute BIBLE STUDY

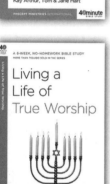

A 6-WEEK, NO-HOMEWORK BIBLE STUDY
MORE THAN 700,000 SOLD IN THE SERIES

Living a
Life of
True Worship

Kay Arthur, Bob & Diane Vereen

PRECEPT MINISTRIES INTERNATIONAL 40minute BIBLE STUDY

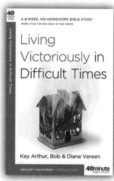

A 6-WEEK, NO-HOMEWORK BIBLE STUDY
MORE THAN 700,000 SOLD IN THE SERIES

Living
Victoriously in
Difficult Times

Kay Arthur, Bob & Diane Vereen

PRECEPT MINISTRIES INTERNATIONAL 40minute BIBLE STUDY

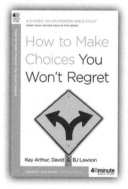

A 6-WEEK, NO-HOMEWORK BIBLE STUDY
MORE THAN 700,000 SOLD IN THE SERIES

How to Make
Choices You
Won't Regret

Kay Arthur, David & BJ Lawson

PRECEPT MINISTRIES INTERNATIONAL 40minute BIBLE STUDY

A 6-WEEK, NO-HOMEWORK BIBLE STUDY
MORE THAN 700,000 SOLD IN THE SERIES

Money and
Possessions:
The Quest for
Contentment

Kay Arthur & David Arthur

PRECEPT MINISTRIES INTERNATIONAL 40minute BIBLE STUDY

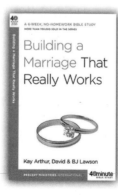

A 6-WEEK, NO-HOMEWORK BIBLE STUDY
MORE THAN 700,000 SOLD IN THE SERIES

Building a
Marriage That
Really Works

Kay Arthur, David & BJ Lawson

PRECEPT MINISTRIES INTERNATIONAL 40minute BIBLE STUDY

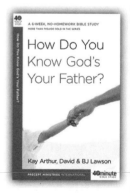

A 6-WEEK, NO-HOMEWORK BIBLE STUDY
MORE THAN 700,000 SOLD IN THE SERIES

How Do You
Know God's
Your Father?

Kay Arthur, David & BJ Lawson

PRECEPT MINISTRIES INTERNATIONAL 40minute BIBLE STUDY

Bible Studies
Discover Truth For Yourself

A 6-WEEK, NO-HOMEWORK BIBLE STUDY
MORE THAN 700,000 SOLD IN THE SERIES

Discovering
What the
Future Holds

Kay Arthur & Georg Huber

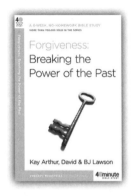
A 6-WEEK, NO-HOMEWORK BIBLE STUDY
MORE THAN 700,000 SOLD IN THE SERIES

Forgiveness:
Breaking the
Power of the Past

Kay Arthur, David & BJ Lawson

A 6-WEEK, NO-HOMEWORK BIBLE STUDY
MORE THAN 700,000 SOLD IN THE SERIES

Living Like
You Belong
to God

Kay Arthur, David & BJ Lawson

A 6-WEEK, NO-HOMEWORK BIBLE STUDY
MORE THAN 700,000 SOLD IN THE SERIES

The Essentials
of Effective
Prayer

Kay Arthur, David & BJ Lawson

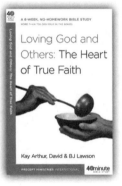
A 6-WEEK, NO-HOMEWORK BIBLE STUDY
MORE THAN 700,000 SOLD IN THE SERIES

Loving God and
Others: The Heart
of True Faith

Kay Arthur, David & BJ Lawson

A 6-WEEK, NO-HOMEWORK BIBLE STUDY
MORE THAN 200,000 SOLD IN THE SERIES

Understanding
Spiritual Gifts

Kay Arthur, David and BJ Lawson

Also Available:
A Man's Strategy for Conquering Temptation
Rising to the Call of Leadership
Key Principles of Biblical Fasting
What Does the Bible Say About Sex?
Turning Your Heart Toward God
Fatal Distractions: Conquering Destructive Temptations
Spiritual Warfare: Overcoming the Enemy
The Power of Knowing God
Breaking Free from Fear

Another powerful study series
from beloved Bible teacher

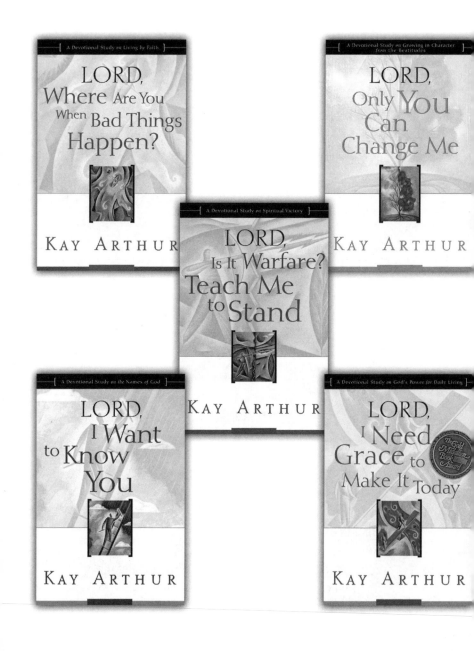

KAY ARTHUR

The Lord series provides insightful, warm-hearted Bible studies designed to meet you where you are—and help you discover God's answers to your deepest needs.

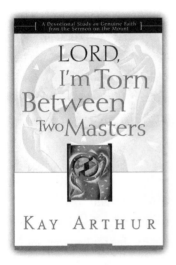

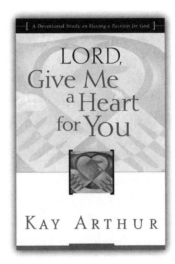

ALSO AVAILABLE:
One-year devotionals to draw you closer to the heart of God.

ABOUT THE AUTHORS AND
PRECEPT MINISTRIES INTERNATIONAL

KAY ARTHUR is known around the world as an international Bible teacher, author, conference speaker, and host of the national radio and television programs *Precepts for Life,* which reaches a worldwide viewing audience of over 94 million. A four-time Gold Medallion Award–winning author, Kay has authored more than 100 books and Bible studies.

Kay and her husband, Jack, founded Precept Ministries International in 1970 in Chattanooga, Tennessee, with a vision to establish people in God's Word. Today, the ministry has a worldwide outreach. In addition to inductive study training workshops and thousands of small-group studies across America, PMI reaches nearly 150 countries with inductive Bible studies translated into nearly 70 languages, teaching people to discover Truth for themselves.

DAVID AND BJ LAWSON have been involved with Precept Ministries International since 1980. After nine years in the pastorate, they joined PMI full-time as directors of the student ministries and staff teachers and trainers. A featured speaker at PMI conferences and in Precept Upon Precept videos, David writes for the Precept Upon Precept series, the New Inductive Study Series, and the 40-Minute Bible Studies series. BJ has written numerous 40-Minute Bible Studies and serves as the chief editor and developer of the series. In addition she is a featured speaker at PMI women's conferences.

Contact Precept Ministries International for more information about inductive Bible studies in your area.

Precept Ministries International
PO Box 182218
Chattanooga, TN 37422-7218
800-763-8280
www.precept.org